Children's Songbag

CHILDREN'S SONGBAG

PAUL DUBOIS JACOBS & JENNIFER SWENDER

Gibbs Smith, Publisher
Salt Lake City

For our parents, with love
—Paul and Jennifer

First Edition
09 08 07 06 05   5 4 3 2 1

Published by
Gibbs Smith, Publisher
P.O. Box 667
Layton, Utah 84041

Orders: 1.800.748.5439
www.gibbs-smith.com

Designed by Dawn DeVries Sokol
Printed and bound in Hong Kong

ISBN 1-58685-356-2

CONTENTS

FOREWORD

PAUL AND JENNIFER have put this wonderful songbag together. May it live and grow with you and your children (and may you mend its seams when frayed).

Have fun.

old Pete

—Pete Seeger

Preface

THE FIRST MUSIC—WHAT WAS IT? An ocean wave? A songbird singing? Two sticks tapping? Somewhere, somehow, someone hummed a tune that got passed around the fire. Presto! The first song!

Since then, songs have been passed down from generation to generation. We've tried to capture a few of them right here in this songbag of children's favorites.

You might ask, "What is a songbag?" Well, just like you have a school bag for your school things and a lunch bag for your lunch, a songbag is a place to keep the songs you care about.

Many of these songs you probably already know. You might even have heard slightly different versions of them than you will see here. Other songs in this book will be new to your ears. We've also included new ways to approach old favorites—look for these tips and tidbits under the headings *Learn more about it!*, *Sing more about it!*, *Did you know?*, *Two for one!*, *Move to it!*, *Cook it!*, and *Read more about it!*

You don't need to read music or play an instrument to enjoy this songbag. But if you do read music, even just a little bit, the magic of two or three simple chords played on a piano or guitar will let you accompany many of the songs in this collection.

If you find a song that's not to your liking, simply skip it. Or better yet, change it around and make it your own. There are always new songs to learn, even if it means taking the tune from one and mixing it with the words from another.

Whether you have a few minutes or a few hours, we hope this book will bring you the joy of singing and music-making. Don't be afraid to sing off-key, whistle, clap your hands, or tap your feet. Keeping music playful and fun is the key to making it a bigger part of our lives. If you really think about it, music can be made anywhere. Just keep an ear open.

So hold on, we're about to take off on a wonderful ride—note-by-note and word-by-word!

Paul   Jennifer

ACKNOWLEDGMENTS

The inspiration for this book was drawn partly from two earlier sources: Carl Sandburg's *The American Songbag* and Ruth Crawford Seeger's *American Folksongs for Children.* We also owe a great deal of debt to the music of Pete Seeger, Lee Hays, Ronnie Gilbert, Fred Hillerman, Peggy Seeger, and Mike Seeger.

The authors would like to thank the following people for their help in cobbling together this book:

Gibbs Smith for entrusting us with his idea; Toshi Seeger for her corn muffins and help with song permissions; Pete Seeger for his song suggestions; Bob Holub and Peter Baldwin for their keen musical eye; Loretta Fellin and Larry Richmond for their patience and assistance; Lloyd Jassin for his "sound" advice; Natalia Jacobs for helping us with typing; and our editor, Jennifer Grillone, for skippering this ship through the publishing sea.

ALL THE PRETTY LITTLE HORSES

Traditional

Learn More about it!

Have you ever wondered what the horses in this traditional American lullaby would look like? Bay horses are red or brown with black manes, tails, and lower legs. Dapples are speckled, usually gray or silver in color. Black horses are black all over with no white markings. And gray horses are just that, but they only turn gray after they lose their baby coat.

Did you Know?

Before the invention of the automobile, people used "horsepower" to get around. Coaches, carriages, buggies, and wagons were all forms of horse-drawn transportation. Some used just one horse, while others involved a team of four, six, or eight horses.

Sing More about it!

Here's the second and less well-known verse of this lullaby. It reveals the sadder side of the song's history. The *wee little lambie* refers to the baby of a slave, whose mother is busy caring for the master's child.

Way down yonder, down in the meadow,
There's a poor wee little lambie,
The bees and the butterflies peckin' out its eyes,
The poor wee thing cried for its mammie.

AMERICA THE BEAUTIFUL

Lyrics by Katherine Lee Bates
Music by Samuel Ward

Oh, beau - ti - ful for spa - cious skies, For

am - ber waves of grain, For pur - ple moun - tains

ma - jes - ty, A - bove the fruit - ed plain! A -

mer - i - ca! A - mer - i - ca! God shed his grace on

thee, And crown thy good with broth - er - hood, From

sea to shin - ing sea!

Learn More About It!

Katherine Lee Bates felt inspired to write about the beauty of her country after a visit to Pike's Peak in Montana. Bates wrote many drafts of her poem before arriving at the final words. Originally, there wasn't any one melody for this song. The tune of the New Year's Eve standard, "Auld Lang Syne," was a favorite. Eventually though, Bates' words were matched up with the melody of "Materna," written by Samuel Ward. That's the song as we know it today.

Sing More About It!

Oh, beautiful for pilgrim feet
Whose stern impassioned stress,
A thoroughfare for freedom beat
Across the wilderness.
America! America!
God mend thine every flaw,
Confirm thy soul in self-control,
Thy liberty in law.

Oh, beautiful for heroes proved
In liberating strife,
Who more than self their country loved
And mercy more than life.
America! America!
May God thy gold refine,
Till all success be nobleness,
And every gain divine.

Oh, beautiful for patriot dream
That sees beyond the years,
Thine alabaster cities gleam
Undimmed by human tears.
America! America!
God shed his grace on thee,
And crown thy good with brotherhood,
From sea to shining sea.

THE BEAR WENT OVER THE MOUNTAIN

Traditional

The bear went o - ver the moun - tain, The

bear went o - ver the moun - tain, The bear went o - ver the

moun - tain to see what he could see, To see what he could

see, __ To see what he could see. __ The oth - er side of the

moun - tain, The oth - er side of the moun - tain, The

oth - er side of the moun - tain was all that he could see.

Learn More about it!

There are eight species of bears, but only five of them would be found going over a mountain. Black bears, brown bears, giant panda bears, Asiatic bears, and spectacled bears all live in mountainous regions of the world. Sun bears and sloth bears, on the other hand, prefer low-lying areas. And polar bears live on the Arctic ice. Chances are the bear went over the mountain to stake out its territory. Bears are very solitary creatures. Unless a mother bear is taking care of her cubs, bears usually live and travel alone.

Two for One!

Try these words to the tune of "The Bear Went Over the Mountain." Does it sound familiar?

For he's a jolly good fellow,
For he's a jolly good fellow,
For he's a jolly good fellow,
That nobody can deny!

BINGO

Traditional

'Twas a farm-er had a dog and Bin-go was his name -O.

B - I -N-G-O, B - I -N-G-O, B - I -

N - G - O, and Bin - go was his name - O!

MOVE TO iT!

Sing this song five times, each time leaving off one letter in Bingo's name and adding a hand clap. By the end, you'll be clapping five times.

DiD YOU KNOW?

These days, Bingo is not one of the most popular dog names. Popular names include Sam, Max, Buddy, Rocky, Daisy, and Duke. Try singing this song with one of these names. Or try singing it using the name of your own dog.

TWO FOR ONE!

Try singing these lyrics to the tune of "Bingo." Any five-letter word will do. Here's a classroom favorite.

It's so nice to see you now,
Let's all say hello-O,
H-E-L-L-O
H-E-L-L-O
H-E-L-L-O
Let's all say hello now.

CRAWLY CREEPY LITTLE MOUSIE

Pete Seeger

Craw - ly   creep - y   lit - tle

mous - ie,   From   the   barn - ie

to   the   hous - ie.   In   the   pan - try

un - der   the   shelf!   He   found   some   cheese   and

helped   him - self.   Nib - ble   nib - ble   Nib - ble   Nib - ble!

Words traditional (nursery rhyme)
Music adapted and arranged by Pete Seeger
Based on the song "Doodle Dandy" collected, adapted and arranged by Frank Warner
TRO – © Copyright 1971 (Renewed), 1984 and 1993 Melody Trails, Inc., New York, NY
Used by Permission

LEARN MORE ABOUT IT!

We learned this song from musician Pete Seeger. The words come from a traditional Scottish nursery rhyme. The tune was adapted from the melody "Doodle Dandy." Try walking your fingers up your arm as you sing the words. Travel over your shoulder and behind your neck, and wind up with a few tickles under your chin when you sing, *Nibble, nibble, nibble, nibble!*

DID YOU KNOW?

Did you know that mice can jump, swim, and climb? And they can squeeze through holes smaller than a dime? Some people even keep mice as pets!

SING MORE ABOUT IT!

Pete Seeger also made up a variation to this song called "Crawly Creepy Little Vine-ee."

Crawly Creepy little vine-ee
'Round the tree goes twisty-twine-ee.
But 'long comes Grandpa with his shears
Snip! He's cutting short your years.

"Not so fast," says little vine-ee.
"You think you've stopped my twisty-twine-ee.
But you just nipped me at the top.
Down below my roots don't stop."

Ah! Through life it's all a struggle.
Enough to make your mind go buggle.
But if we can laugh and make up rhymes
We might live a longer time!

Do Your Ears Hang Low?

Traditional

Do your ears hang low? Do they

wob - ble to and fro? Can you tie them in a knot? Can you

tie them in a bow? Can you throw them o'er your shoul -der like a

con - ti - nen -tal sol - dier? Do your ears hang low?

LEARN MORE ABOUT IT!

A continental soldier was an American soldier fighting against the British in the American Revolutionary War. Continental soldiers wore three-cornered hats called *tricorns*. The hats had three flaps that could be worn up or down. Soldiers often wore one of the side flaps down to protect their ear and shoulder when firing a musket. Perhaps this explains the song line, *Can you throw them over your shoulder like a continental soldier?*

SING MORE ABOUT IT!

Here's a verse we made up. Try making up your own verses using feet, elbows, shoulders, or toes.

Do your hands reach high?
Can they touch the sky?
Are they long and thin
for a tickle under the chin?
Can you shake 'em up and down?
Can you wave 'em all around?
Do your hands reach high?

Down at the Station

Traditional

Down at the sta - tion ear - ly in the morn - ing,

See the lit - tle puff - er - bel - lies all in a row,

See the en - gine dri - ver pull the lit - tle han - dle,

Toot - toot, Puff - puff, Off they go!

Learn More about it!

You may have seen this song called "Down by the Station." This is a song about an old-fashioned train called a *steam locomotive*. These trains were powered by steam created by boiling water using either wood or coal. The more steam pressure, the faster the train would go. It was the engineer's job to pull the throttle (or what's called the *handle* in the song). The throttle was the valve that allowed the engineer to control the amount of pressure between the engine and the boiler. The fireman, or stoker, was responsible for keeping the fire going.

Read More about it!

Interested in trains? Check out these favorite books:

The Little Engine That Could by Watty Piper
Freight Train by Donald Crews
Two Little Trains by Margaret Wise Brown
The Polar Express by Chris Van Allsburg

DOWN BY THE BAY

Traditional

LeaRN MoRe about it!

Watermelon is a favorite treat for a Fourth of July picnic. Watermelons are over 90 percent water. They grow best in sandy soil and warm weather. Believe it or not, watermelons were first grown five thousand years ago in Egypt. They even made it into the first cookbook published in Colonial America, which contained a recipe for pickled watermelon rind.

DiD you kNow?

In some parts of the world watermelon seeds are toasted and salted and eaten as a snack just like peanuts.

SiNg MoRe about it!

This is a *call and response song*. One person sings the first line. The rest of the group sings back the response (the part in parentheses). Find two words that rhyme and try making up your own verse to this silly song. Here are some examples:

Did you ever see . . . a bear combing its hair?
　　　　　　　　　a fly wearing a tie?
　　　　　　　　　llamas eating their pajamas?
(Did you ever have a time when you couldn't make a rhyme?)

Eency Weency Spider

Traditional

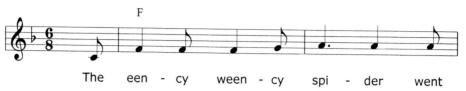

The een - cy ween - cy spi - der went

up the wa - ter spout, Down came the rain and

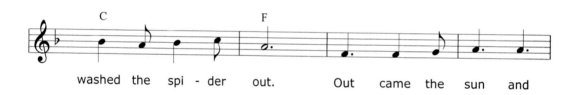

washed the spi - der out. Out came the sun and

dried up all the rain, And the een - cy ween - cy

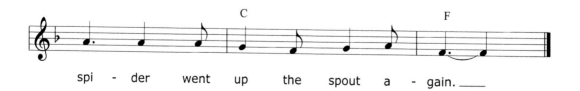

spi - der went up the spout a - gain. ____

Learn More about it!

The smallest spider in the world is no bigger than the head of a pin. The largest, the goliath tarantula, is as big as a dinner plate. Yikes! If you see a spider climbing up your waterspout, it's most likely a daddy longlegs, one of the most common spiders.

The spider in this song lives *near* water, but some spiders live *under* water! They are called diving water spiders. Instead of a tank of air on their backs, these spiders carry trapped air bubbles underneath their bellies. In fact, these diving spiders can spend most of their lives under water even though they breathe air just like us!

Read More about it!

If you like spiders, you might enjoy these books:

Little Miss Spider by David Kirk

The Very Busy Spider by Eric Carle

Aaaarrgghh, Spider! by Lydia Monks

Move to it!

You can do hand movements to go along with this song. When you sing *went up the water spout,* use two fingers on your right hand and walk them up your left arm. When you sing *down came the rain,* put your hands high above your head and wiggle your fingers while bringing your hands down to your sides. When you sing *out came the sun,* put your hands above your head and wave them from side to side.

FARMER IN THE DELL

Traditional

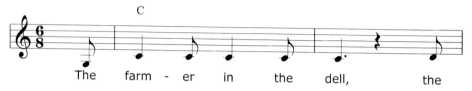

The farm - er in the dell, the

farm - er in the dell,

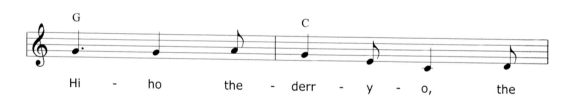

Hi - ho the - derr - y - o, the

farm - er in the dell.

Learn More about it!

This song is based on a traditional German folk song. A dell is a ravine or small valley, usually covered by trees, brush, or grass.

Sing More about it!

Here's the rest of the song. Each verse introduces a new character.

The farmer takes a wife . . .
The wife takes a child . . .
The child takes a nurse . . .
The nurse takes a dog . . .
The dog takes a cat . . .
The cat takes a rat . . .
The rat takes the cheese . . .
The cheese stands alone.

Move To it!

Try this simple dance game. Everybody stands in a circle and joins hands. The farmer stands in the middle while the group sings and circles around. Then the farmer chooses someone to be a wife. The wife joins the farmer in the middle and the group sings and circles around again. Repeat this for each verse of the song. At the end, whoever is picked as the cheese gets to be the farmer in the next round.

FIVE LITTLE DUCKS

Traditional

Five lit - tle ducks went out one day,

O - ver the hills and far a ___ - way, Ma - ma duck said "Quack,

quack, quack, quack," But on - ly four lit - tle ducks came back.

DiD you KNOW?

Ducks can lay as many as ten to twelve eggs, and it takes about a month for the ducklings to hatch. When they do, mother ducks keep the ducklings close by to protect them. If a group of geese is called a gaggle, what do you call a group of ducks? A paddling!

TWO FOR ONE!

There are many game songs that count down from five to one, each with a different melody. Here are just a few.

Five little speckled frogs
Sat on a speckled log,
Eating the most delicious bugs,
One jumped into the pool
Where it was nice and cool,
Then there were four green speckled frogs!
Four little speckled frogs . . .

Five little monkeys jumping on the bed,
One fell off and bumped his head,
Mama called the doctor and the doctor said,
"No more monkeys jumping on the bed!"
Four little monkeys . . .

What about counting down from ten to one!

There were ten in the bed and the little one said,
"Roll over! Roll over!"
So they all rolled over and one fell off.
There were nine in the bed and the little one said . . .

FRÈRE JACQUES

Traditional

Fre - re   Jac - ques,   Fre - re   Jac - ques,   Dor - mez - vous?

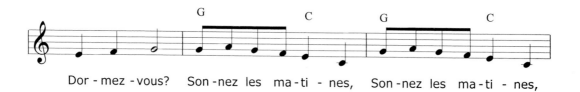

Dor - mez - vous?   Son - nez les ma - ti - nes,   Son - nez les ma - ti - nes,

Din,   din,   don,   Din,   din,   don.

Learn More about It!

This traditional French song is commonly sung as a *round*. In a round, one singer begins the song and is joined a few measures later by another singer, then another. Each new singer starts at the beginning and sings all the way through. This way, each part of the song is always being sung by one singer or another.

The morning bells in this song probably refer to church bells chiming to mark the hour. Bells have been used throughout history for keeping time and signaling special events. This was especially true before people had watches and clocks of their own.

Sing More about It!

Here's the English-language version of the song.

Are you sleeping? Are you sleeping?
Brother John, Brother John,
Morning bells are ringing,
Morning bells are ringing,
Ding, ding, dong, ding, ding, dong.

The Green Grass Grew All Around

Traditional

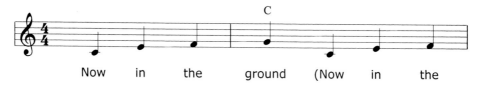

Now in the ground (Now in the

ground), There was a hole (There was a

hole), The pretti-est lit-tle hole (The pretti-est lit-tle

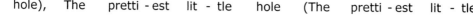

hole), That you ev-er did see (That you ev-er did see). Oh, the

hole in the ground and the green grass grew all a -

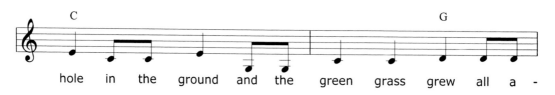

round, all a-round, and the green grass grew all a-round.

Sing More about it!

This is a *cumulative song*. Each verse takes the song one step further. It's also a *call and response song*. The lead singer sings a line, which the chorus echoes. The chorus's part is in parentheses.

Now in that hole (Now in that hole),
There was a tree (There was a tree),
The prettiest little tree (The prettiest little tree)
That you ever did see (That you ever did see).
Oh, the tree in the hole,
And the hole in the ground,
And the green grass grew all around, all
*   around,*
And the green grass grew all around.

Now on that tree (Now on that tree),
There was a branch (There was a branch),
The prettiest little branch (The prettiest
*   little branch)*
That you ever did see (That you ever did see).
Oh, the branch on the tree
And the tree in the hole . . .

Continue with the verses below. It's a long song!

Now on that branch, there was a limb . . .
Now on that limb, there was a twig . . .
Now on that twig, there was a nest . . .
Now in that nest, there was a bird . . .
Now on that bird, there was a feather . . .
Now on that feather, there was a flea . . .

HE'S GOT THE WHOLE WORLD

Traditional

He's got the whole world in his hands. He's got the

whole wide world in his hands. He's got the whole world

in his hands. He's got the whole world in his hands.

Learn More About It!

Like so many early songs, this song has religious origins. However, today children and adults enjoy singing it no matter their religious beliefs. It's particularly popular in summer camps, where the simplicity of its lyrics invites everyone to join in.

Sing More About It!

One great thing about this song is that it's easy to make up a lot of verses. Here are a few to get you started, but feel free to create even more.

He's got the mommies and the daddies in his hands . . .
He's got the brothers and the sisters in his hands . . .
He's got the little bitty babies in his hands . . .
He's got the doggies and the kitties in his hands . . .
He's got the frogs and the toads in his hands . . .

Two For One!

In many schools, this song has become popular for Earth Day celebrations. A small change in the lyrics reminds us of the responsibility we all have to take care of our planet.

We've got the whole world in our hands . . .
We've got the air and the water in our hands . . .
We've got the birds and the fish in our hands . . .
We've got the trees and the rivers in our hands . . .

Hush, Li'l Baby

Traditional

Hush, lit - tle ba - by don't say a word,

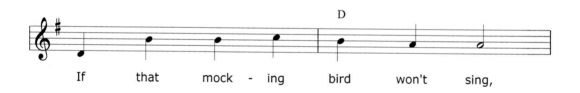

Pa - pa's gon - na buy you a mock - ing bird.

If that mock - ing bird won't sing,

Pa - pa's gon - na buy you a dia - mond ring.

Collected, adapted and arranged by John A. Lomax and Alan Lomax
TRO – © Copyright 1941 (Renewed) Ludlow Music, Inc., New York, NY
Used by Permission

LEARN MORE ABOUT IT!

This song, also known as "The Mockingbird Song," seems to be an American version of an old English lullaby. In some versions, it's Mama instead of Papa who buys the mockingbird and all the other gifts . . . but only if the baby goes to sleep!

SING MORE ABOUT IT!

If that diamond ring turns brass,
Papa's gonna buy you a looking glass.

If that looking glass gets broke,
Papa's gonna buy you a billy goat.

If that billy goat won't pull,
Papa's gonna buy you a cart and bull.

If that cart and bull turn over,
Papa's gonna buy you a dog named Rover.

If that dog named Rover don't bark,
Papa's gonna buy you a horse and cart.

If that horse and cart fall down,
You'll still be the prettiest little baby in town.

I Had a Rooster

Traditional

I had a roost-er and the roost-er pleased me, I

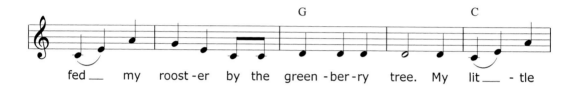

fed __ my roost-er by the green-ber-ry tree. My lit __ - tle

roost-er went cock - a - doo - dle - doo, dee - doo - dle - ee -

doo - dle - ee - doo - dle - ee - doo.

Did You Know?

Why do roosters crow in the morning? Actually, roosters crow at all times of the day, but they are most active in the early hours. This love of the morning is true for all birds. It has to do with territory. Think of the rooster's crowing as a sign posting: "THIS IS MY BARNYARD!"

Sing More about It!

This song is a *cumulative song*. With each animal, the chorus gets longer and longer. Add as many animals as you want. The only limit is your imagination.

I had a hen and the hen pleased me,
I fed my hen by the greenberry tree,
My little hen went cluck, cluck, cluck,
My little rooster went cock-a-doodle-doo,
Dee-doodle-ee-doodle-ee-doodle-ee-doo.

I had a pig and the pig pleased me,
I fed my pig by the greenberry tree,
My little pig went oink, oink, oink,
My little hen went cluck, cluck, cluck,
My little rooster went cock-a-doodle-doo,
Dee-doodle-ee-doodle-ee-doodle-ee-doo.

I had a cow and the cow pleased me,
I fed my cow by the greenberry tree,
My little cow went moo, moo, moo,
My little pig went oink, oink, oink,
My little hen went cluck, cluck, cluck,
My little rooster went cock-a-doodle-doo,
Dee-doodle-ee-doodle-ee-doodle-ee-doo.

IF YOU'RE HAPPY AND YOU KNOW IT

Traditional

If you're hap-py and you know it, clap your hands!

If you're hap-py and you know it, clap your hands!

If you're hap-py and you know it, and you reall-y want to

show it, If you're hap-py and you know it, clap your hands!

LEARN MORE ABOUT IT!

This popular classroom song supposedly borrows its tune from an old church hymn. This kind of borrowing was common among old songs. People simply took a popular tune or hymn, put new words to it, and presto! A new song!

SING MORE ABOUT IT!

What is your favorite thing to do when you are happy? Here are a few verses to get you started.

If you're happy and you know it,
Stamp your feet!

If you're happy and you know it,
Shout hooray!

If you're happy and you know it,
Jump up and down!

MOVE TO IT!

When you sing this song, do the actions to go along with it. After the song says *clap your hands,* then clap two times. The same for stomping your feet, shouting hooray, and whatever other verses and actions you add to it.

I'M A LITTLE TEAPOT

Traditional

I'm a lit - tle tea - pot, short and stout,

Here is my han - dle, Here is my spout.

When I get all steamed up, Hear me shout,

Tip me o - ver and pour me out.

MOVE TO iT!

Many people know the motions to this popular song. When you sing, *Here is my handle,* put one hand on your hip to form a handle with your elbow. When you sing, *Here is my spout,* put your other arm straight out to the side. And when you sing, *Tip me over and pour me out,* bend to the side with your straight arm as far as you can.

COOK iT!

Invite over some friends and have your own tea party.

SUN TEA

large glass jar or pitcher

4 or 5 tea bags

1–2 quarts of cold water

1 lemon

sugar

ice

Soak tea bags in a pitcher of water. Place pitcher in a sunny spot, like on a windowsill. Let the sun "brew" your tea for 2 to 3 hours. Add a squeeze of lemon, sugar to taste, and ice. Serve with your favorite cookies or other treats.

I'VE BEEN WORKING ON THE RAILROAD

Traditional

I've been working on the rail-road, all the live-long

day. I've been work-ing on the rail-road, just to

pass the time a - way. Can't you hear the whis-tle

blow - ing? Rise up so ear-ly in the morn.

Can't you hear the cap-tain shout-ing, "Di - nah, blow your

horn?" Di - nah won't you blow, Di - nah won't you blow,

Di - nah won't you blow your horn? _____ Di - nah won't you blow,

Di - nah won't you blow, Di - nah won't you blow your horn?

Some - one's in the kitch - en with Di - nah,

Some - one's in the kitch - en I know. _____

Some - one's in the kitch - en with Di - nah,

Strum - ming on the old ban - jo and sing - ing, Fee - fi -

I'VE BEEN WORKING ON THE RAILROAD

(CONTINUED)

fid - lee - i - o, Fee - fi - fid - lee - i - o, _____ Fee - fi -

fid - lee - i - o, Strum-ming on the old ban - jo!

LEARN MORE ABOUT IT!

A lot of backbreaking work went into laying railroad track—especially during the days in America when people were first moving west. *Work songs* were often used to help people forget how tired and sore they were. Some people think "I've Been Working on the Railroad" was first sung by Irish workmen, who sang it as "I've been working on the levee." Other people think it started as an African-American song called "The Levee Song." A levee is a bank—a small hill really—built up along a river to keep it from overflowing.

If you're wondering why the workers want Dinah to blow her horn, it's because horns were often used to call workers to lunch, especially if the workforce was spread out over a wide area. This was in the days long before cell phones and intercoms.

Train travel has come a long way since those first early railroad tracks were laid. Gone are the old steam locomotives throwing up billowing smoke. Now, bullet trains like those in Japan and France are famous for their high speeds.

If you're interested in old trains, you can visit the California State Railroad Museum in Old Sacramento, or the Railroad Museum of Pennsylvania in Strasburg. And if you'd like to ride a train straight up a mountain, you can take the coal-driven Cog Railway up to the summit of New Hampshire's Mount Washington. Or there may be a railroad museum near you.

LITTLE BIRD, LITTLE BIRD

Traditional

Lit - tle bird, lit - tle bird, fly through my win - dow,

Lit - tle bird, lit - tle bird, fly through my win - dow,

Lit - tle bird, lit - tle bird, fly through my win - dow, And

buy mo -lass -es can - dy. Fly through my win -dow my su -gar lump, Fly

through my win -dow my su -gar lump, And buy mo -lass -es can - dy.

LEARN MORE ABOUT IT!

How many different kinds of birds do you know? Instead of singing "little bird, little bird," substitute the name of a bird you see around your neighborhood. If you live in the city, you might sing about a pigeon. If you live in the country, you might sing about a crow or a robin. Here's how it might go, *Pigeon, pigeon, fly through my window . . .*

COOK IT!

If you'd like to try a bit of molasses candy, have an adult help you with this recipe.

OLD-FASHIONED MOLASSES CANDY

1 cup molasses

2 cups brown sugar

3 tablespoons vinegar

½ to 1 cup of water

2 tablespoons butter

Mix the molasses, sugar, vinegar, and water in a saucepan over medium heat. Make sure the sugar dissolves. To test, drop a spoonful of the mixture in a cup of cold water. It should be brittle enough to break. Pour the mixture into a pan. When the mixture is cool, rub butter on both your hands, then stretch and pull the candy until it is light brown in color. Cut into pieces.

LONDON BRIDGE

Traditional

Lon - don Bridge is fall - ing down,

fall - ing down, fall - ing down, Lon - don Bridge is

fall - ing down, My fair la - dy.

LEARN MORE ABOUT IT!

London Bridge! Tradition says that a bridge has been on this site (or near to it) over the River Thames for the past two thousand years. Early London bridges were made of wood. They burned down, rotted, or simply washed away. The first bridge made out of stone was built in 1209. That bridge lasted six hundred years. In the first half of the nineteenth century, a new bridge was constructed, but with one small problem—it kept sinking! In 1970, it was taken down and sold. It's now in Arizona. If you happen to be in London, you can visit the current London Bridge. That bridge opened in 1973.

SING MORE ABOUT IT!

Here's verse two:

Take a key and lock her up, lock her up,
  lock her up,
Take a key and lock her up,
My fair lady.

MOVE TO IT!

Try this simple dance. Two dancers join both hands and raise their arms to create a bridge. The other dancers pass under the bridge as they sing the song. But be careful! When you sing *take a key and lock her up,* the arms of the bridge come down. Whoever is inside is stuck!

LOOBY LOO

Traditional

You put your right hand in, You put your right hand

out, You give your hand a shake, shake, shake, and

turn your-self a - bout. Here we go loo - by loo,

here we go loo - by light, Here we go loo - by

loo, All on a Sa - tur - day night.

Learn More about it!

Saturday nights are still popular nights for dances and fun. However, some people think this song is simply about a Saturday evening bath! The lyrics about putting your hands, legs, and whole self *in* is supposedly about dipping parts of your body into the bath water.

Sing More about it!

You don't have to follow these verses exactly. Any part of your body will do.

You put your left hand in . . .
You put your right foot in . . .
You put your left foot in . . .
You put your right elbow in . . .
You put your left elbow in . . .
You put your whole self in . . .

Two for One!

The words and motions to this song might remind you of another singing game, "The Hokey Pokey." Go ahead and try it out!

You put your right hand in,
You take your right hand out,
You put your right hand in,
And you shake it all about,
You do the hokey pokey,
And you turn yourself around,
That's what it's all about!

MARY HAD A LITTLE LAMB

Sarah Josepha Hale

Ma - ry had a lit - tle lamb, lit - tle lamb,

lit - tle lamb. Ma - ry had a lit - tle lamb whose

fleece was white as snow.

LEARN MORE ABOUT IT!

Some people say the words to this song were first written by a New Hampshire man named John Roulstone. However, another author, Sarah Josepha Hale, published the song in 1830, claiming the words as her own. There is an even earlier British rhyme about Lucy and her little lamb. Whichever story is true, there's no doubt that this *nursery rhyme* was part of a major milestone in history. In 1877, the first recording of a human voice was inventor Thomas Edison reciting "Mary Had a Little Lamb."

TWO FOR ONE!

Try these words to the tune of "Mary Had a Little Lamb." They are part of another song called "Goodnight Ladies."

Merrily we roll along, roll along, roll along,
Merrily we roll along over the deep blue sea.

Mary Wore Her Red Dress

Traditional

Ma - ry wore her red dress,

red dress, red dress,

Ma - ry wore her red dress,

all day long.

LEARN MORE ABOUT IT!

This classic American folk song is a favorite in schools everywhere. The pleasant melody and simple lyrics make it an easy song to sing—and change!

SING MORE ABOUT IT!

Try changing the words to create as many verses as you have clothes in your closet.

Emma wore her blue hat, blue hat, blue hat . . .

Jacob wore his soccer cleats, soccer cleats, soccer cleats . . .

Don't be afraid to change the song even more!

Jesse read a long book, long book, long book . . .

Bella got a new dog, new dog, new dog . . .

Michael Row The Boat Ashore

Traditional

Mich - ael row the boat a - shore, Hal - le -

lu - jah! Mich - ael row the boat a -

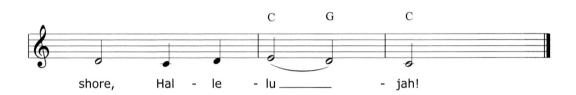

shore, Hal - le - lu _____ - jah!

Learn More About It!

This song is both a *spiritual* and a *work song*. A work song helped people work together. Sometimes that work was rowing, which required exact timing so that everyone pulled the oars exactly together.

You might wonder why the song asks Sister to *trim the sails*. *Trim* is a sailing term. It means adjust the sails to catch the wind.

The third and fourth verses of this song refer to the famous Jordan River of the Middle East. The river starts in Northern Israel and empties into the Dead Sea. Besides providing much-needed water to a dry, desert landscape, the Jordan River holds a special place in the history of three of the world's major religions: Christianity, Judaism, and Islam.

Sing More About It!

Sister help to trim the sails, Hallelujah!
Sister help to trim the sails, Hallelujah!

Jordan's River is deep and wide, Hallelujah!
Milk and honey on the other side, Hallelujah!

Jordan's River is chilly and cold, Hallelujah!
Chills the body but not the soul, Hallelujah!

MISTER RABBIT

Traditional

Mis - ter Rab - bit, Mis - ter Rab - bit, your

ears are might - y long. Yes, my Lord, they were

put on wrong. _ Ev ___ - 'ry lit - tle soul's gon -na shine, shine. _

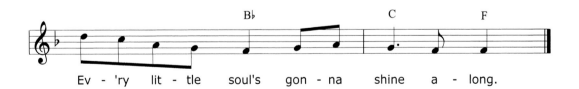

Ev - 'ry lit - tle soul's gon - na shine a - long.

LEARN MORE ABOUT IT!

Rabbits come in all shapes and sizes. Some have long hair, some short hair. Some are big, some small. Some have ears that stand up, while others have ears that flop down. And, of course, rabbits come in all kinds of colors. Some people say this song is simply about a quick-talking rabbit trying to escape from a farmer. Others say it's about accepting people for who they are. What do you think?

SING MORE ABOUT IT!

Here are the rest of the verses.

Mister Rabbit, Mister Rabbit,
Your coat's mighty gray,
Yes, my Lord, it was made that way.

Mister Rabbit, Mister Rabbit,
You're ears are mighty thin,
Yes, that's because they're splittin' in the wind.

Mister Rabbit, Mister Rabbit,
Your tail is mighty white,
Yes, my Lord, and I'm goin' out of sight.

Mister Rabbit, Mister Rabbit,
You're in my cabbage patch,
Yes, my Lord, and I won't come back.

The Muffin Man

Traditional

Do you know the muf - fin man, the

muf - fin man, the muf - fin man?

Do you know the muf - fin man who

lives on Dru - ry Lane?

LEaRN MoRE aBout iT!

Nobody really knows who the muffin man was, but Drury Lane is a street in the city of London. The street is famous for being home to the Drury Lane Theater, the oldest English theater still in use. It opened in 1663. That's more than a hundred years before the United States came into existence!

COOK iT!

You can add just about anything to these muffins: blueberries, strawberries, or bananas. Your taste buds are the limit.

SIMPLE MUFFINS

1 cup flour

½ teaspoon salt

½ cup sugar

1 teaspoon baking powder

1 egg

2 tablespoons butter

⅓ cup milk

fruit of your choice

Melt butter and set aside to cool. Mix together flour, salt, sugar, and baking powder. In a medium bowl, beat egg and add milk and melted butter. Add fruit. Spoon batter into a greased muffin pan. Bake at 375 degrees for 15 minutes.

The Mulberry Bush

Traditional

Here we go 'round the mul - ber - ry bush, the

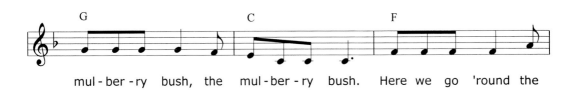

mul - ber - ry bush, the mul - ber - ry bush. Here we go 'round the

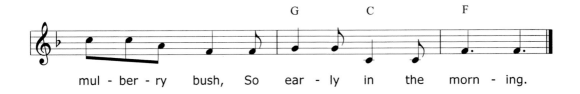

mul - ber - ry bush, So ear - ly in the morn - ing.

LEARN MORE ABOUT IT!

Don't believe this song! Mulberries grow on trees, not bushes. The berries are similar to blackberries or loganberries, and can be used to make jellies and jams. Mulberries are not as popular as other fruits because they spoil quickly.

TWO FOR ONE!

Here's another popular verse that features a mulberry bush. Do you recognize it?

All around the mulberry bush,
The monkey chased the weasel,
The monkey thought 'twas all in fun,
Pop goes the weasel!

MOVE TO IT!

Try singing this song the next time you play musical chairs. Put all of the chairs in a circle facing out, with one less chair than the number of people playing the game. Walk or dance around them as you sing, *Here we go 'round the mulberry bush.* Remember, when the song ends, you need to find a place to sit down!

Oh, Susanna

Stephen Foster

I ___ come from Al - a - ba - ma with my

ban - jo on my knee, I am goin' to Lou - 'si -

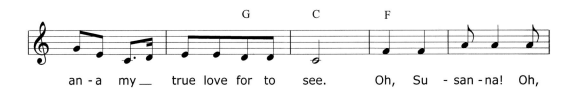

an - a my ___ true love for to see. Oh, Su - san - na! Oh,

don't you cry for me, for I come from A - la -

ba - ma with my ban - jo on my knee.

LEARN MORE ABOUT IT!

"Oh, Susanna" was written by the nineteenth-century American songwriter Stephen Foster. You have probably heard some of Foster's other famous songs like "Camptown Races" and "The Old Folks at Home" (also known as "Swanee River"). Foster's songs were as popular in his lifetime as they are today. However, in the days before radios and CDs, Foster was dependent on the sale of sheet music to earn a living. It is said he only earned about $15,000 from his music. Today, someone as famous as he was would be a millionaire.

SING MORE ABOUT IT!

Here's the silly second verse of this song. See if you can make any sense of it.

It rained all night the day I left,
The weather was bone dry,
The sun so hot I froze myself,
Susanna don't you cry.

OLD MacDonald

Traditional

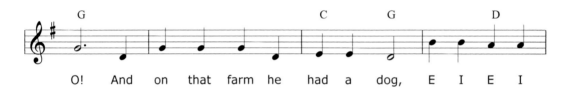

Old Mac - Don - ald had a farm, E - I - E - I -

O! And on that farm he had a dog, E I E I

O! With a woof - woof here and a woof - woof there,

Here a woof, there a woof, Ev - 'ry - where a woof - woof!

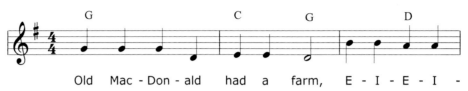

Old Mac - Don - ald had a farm, E - I - E - I - O!

DiD you KNOW?

Here are some fun facts about farms.

- The largest chicken egg on record weighed nearly ¾ of a pound.
- A dairy cow can supply over 200,000 glasses of milk in her lifetime.
- Cats with white fur on their faces can sunburn.
- Miniature potbellied pigs can be trained to use a litter box and leash, and can be kept as pets.
- There are more chickens in the world than human beings.

SiNG MORE aBOUT iT!

There are many verses to this song. Here are a few suggestions.

On that farm he had a chick, with a cheep-cheep here . . .
On that farm he had a duck, with a quack-quack here . . .
On that farm he had a cat, with a meow-meow here . . .
On that farm he had a pig, with an oink-oink here . . .
On that farm he had a cow, with a moo-moo here . . .

What other animals can you think of?

ON TOP OF OLD SMOKEY

Traditional

On top of old Smo - key, _____

___ All cov - ered with snow, _____

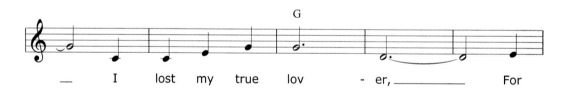

___ I lost my true lov - er, _____ For

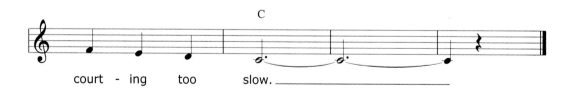

court - ing too slow. _____

Learn More about it!

This is a popular camp song, and like a lot of old songs, the lyrics to "Old Smokey" are a little silly. Did somebody lose their love in a mountain snowstorm? Or did the two parts of the song come from different versions written by different people?

If you're interested in climbing Old Smokey, you have a couple of choices. There's Smokey Peak in Arizona, and Old Smokey Mountain in Newfoundland, Canada. There are also the famous (and quite beautiful) Smokey Mountains on the border of Tennessee and North Carolina.

Sing More about it

Some of you might be familiar with another version of this song called "On Top of Spaghetti." This hilarious tune by songwriter Tom Glaser uses the same melody, but different words.

Here are a few verses that we made up using the tune of "Old Smokey."

On top of the leaf pile, all covered with leaves,
I lost my poor brother when he dived in between.

On top of the bunk bed, all covered with sheets,
I lost my old teddy, way down by my feet.

OVER IN THE MEADOW

Traditional

O - ver in the mead - ow, in the

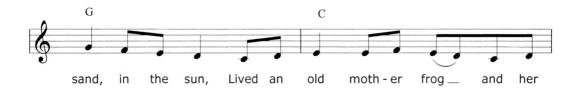

sand, in the sun, Lived an old moth - er frog __ and her

lit - tle frog - gie one. "Croak!" said the moth - er, "I

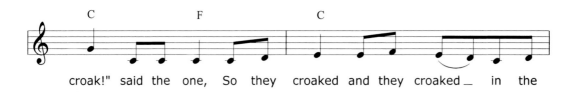

croak!" said the one, So they croaked and they croaked __ in the

sand in the sun.

LEARN MORE ABOUT IT!

This *counting song* is a classroom favorite. The first verse starts with one and each verse adds a number until you reach ten. There are many versions, but they all take place in a meadow and share a common theme of counting up to ten. A meadow is like a field, a wide open area with mostly tall grasses and sometimes flowers.

SING MORE ABOUT IT!

Here are a few verses to get you counting, but try making up your own.

Over in the meadow in the stream so blue,
Lived an old mother fish and her little fishes two.
"Swim!" said the mother. "We swim!" said the two.
And they swam and they swam in the stream so blue.

Over in the meadow on the branch of a tree,
Lived an old mother bird and her little birdies three.
"Sing!" said the mother. "We sing!" said the three.
So they sang and they sang on the branch of a tree.

READ MORE ABOUT IT!

Over in the Meadow by Ezra Jack Keats
Over in the Ocean: In a Coral Reef by Marianne Burkes
Over in the Grasslands by Anna Wilson

Ring Around The Rosie

Traditional

Ring   a - round   the   ro - sie,   pock - et   full   of

po   -   sie,   Ash   -   es,   ash   -   es,   we

all   fall   down! _____

Learn More About It!

This song is perhaps one of the most popular in this book. Nearly everyone sings or has heard "Ring Around the Rosie." Some people believe that the words of the song refer to a deadly plague in Europe in the 1300s. Others believe this song is simply an innocent children's rhyme. Early versions of the song contain more lighthearted lyrics. Here are a few examples.

Ring-a-ring o' roses,
A pocket full of posies,
One for Jack, and one for Jim,
And one for little Moses.
A-tischa! A-tischa! A-tischa!

Ring, a ring o' roses,
A pocket full o' posies,
Upstairs and downstairs,
In my lady's chamber—
Husher! Husher! Cuckoo!

Move to It!

Most of us are familiar with the movements that accompany this song. But just in case you aren't, here are the basics: All of the dancers take hands to form a circle. Dancers walk or skip in one direction until the end of the song, when everyone falls down!

Sing More About It!

Try changing the words to include the names of your friends. One person stands in the middle of the circle. Get ready to come up with some rhymes!

Ring around Sandy,
Pocket full of candy . . .

Ring around Shelley,
Pocket full of jelly . . .

Rock-a-Bye Baby

Traditional

Rock - a - bye ba - by on the tree top,

When the wind blows, the cra - dle will rock. When the bough

breaks, the cra - dle will fall, And down will come

ba - by, cra - dle and all!

LEARN MORE ABOUT IT!

This song is a *lullaby*. A lullaby is a quiet, soothing song that is sung to put a child to sleep. But the words to this song hardly seem comforting—a baby falling from a tree! Some people believe the words describe a Native American practice of resting babies on cradle boards in the limbs of trees. The wind could gently rock the babies to sleep while their mothers worked nearby.

DID YOU KNOW?

Did you know that newborns need 14 to 18 hours of sleep a day? But not all living things sleep alike. Horses need only $2^1/_2$ to 3 hours of sleep a day, while monkeys need about 10 hours. Adult humans function best with 8 hours. Ducks, amazingly enough, can use half their brain for sleep, while the other half stays alert.

Row, Row, Row Your Boat

Traditional

Row, row, row your boat, Gent - ly down the

stream, Mer - ri - ly, mer - ri - ly, mer - ri - ly, mer - ri - ly,

Life is but a dream.

LEaRN MoRE aBout iT!

There are several ways to row your boat down a stream. For the "sailor's row," each oar is pulled one at a time. A more common technique is to row both oars at once. This keeps the boat on the straight and narrow.

DiD you KNoW?

Rowboats have been around for thousands of years. Today, rowing has evolved into a popular sport. It's even a part of the summer Olympics. The first book on rowing was published in Philadelphia in 1836, titled *Walker's Manly Exercises.*

MoVE To iT!

Try this movement game. First, think of a way to change the song to a different mode of transportation. Then act out the motion of that activity. Have your friends guess your new way of traveling. You might *Drive, drive, drive your car* by moving your hands like they're on the steering wheel, or *Pedal, pedal, pedal your bike* by pedaling with your feet.

She'll Be Comin' 'Round The Mountain

Traditional

She'll be com-in' round the moun-tain when she

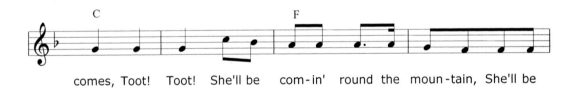

comes, Toot! Toot! She'll be com-in' round the moun-tain when she

comes, Toot! Toot! She'll be com-in' round the moun-tain, She'll be

com-in' round the moun-tain, She'll be com-in' round the

mean-tain when she comes. Toot! Toot!

LEARN MORE ABOUT IT!

This early railroad song has many different versions and is a favorite among children and adults alike. Train travel back in the nineteenth century was still quite new, and the arrival of a relative from far away was always a special occasion. This might help explain the excitement and playfulness in this song.

SING MORE ABOUT IT!

Here are a few verses to get you started on your journey.

She'll be driving six white horses when she comes,
Whoa back!

She'll be wearing pink pajamas when she comes,
Scratch, scratch!

We'll all go out to meet her when she comes,
Hi, Babe!

We'll all have chicken and dumplings when
she comes,
Yum, yum!

She'll have to sleep with grandma when she
comes,
Snore, snore!

MOVE TO IT!

Try adding a motion to each of the lines. For example, on the *Toot, toot!* pull your fist down for the train whistle. For the *Whoa back!* pretend you're reigning in six white horses. Rub your belly for the *Yum, yum!*

Shoo Fly

Traditional

Shoo fly don't both - er me, Shoo fly don't

both - er me, Shoo fly don't both - er me, I be - long to

some - bod - y. I feel, I feel, I feel like a morn - ing

star. I feel, I feel, I feel like a morn - ing star.

DiD YOU KNOW?

You might find flies a bother, but before you shoo them away, you should know that flies can be very helpful. They transfer pollen between plants, and they are an important part of the food chain. Flies also have special eyes called "compound eyes," which can contain as many as 4,000 lenses. And if a fly is really bothering you, just be patient. They only live for about twenty days.

COOK IT!

Don't worry, Shoo Fly Pie does not have flies in it! However, if placed on a windowsill to cool, this sugary, sticky dessert quickly attracts flies, which is where it got its name.

SHOO FLY PIE

½ cup flour

½ cup brown sugar

⅓ cup butter or shortening

½ cup molasses

½ cup hot water

½ teaspoon baking soda

1 pie shell

Using a fork, in a medium-sized bowl mix together the flour, sugar, and butter to form a crumble. In another bowl, combine the molasses, water, and baking soda, and pour into an uncooked pie shell. Sprinkle the crumble on top. Bake at 375 degrees for 30 minutes.

Skip To My Lou

Traditional

Skip,   skip,   skip   to   my   Lou,

Skip,   skip,   skip   to   my   Lou,

Skip,   skip,   skip   to   my   Lou,

Skip   to   my   Lou,   my   dar - ling.

LEARN MORE ABOUT IT!

When this song became popular on the western frontier, dancing was often forbidden for religious reasons. However, *singing games* like "Skip to My Lou" were allowed. You could sing and clap to your heart's content, as long as you didn't dance or play musical instruments.

SING MORE ABOUT IT!

There are many, many verses to this popular song. Some of them are very simple, as if people were singing about whatever was right in front of them. Try making up a few of your own verses.

Cat's in the cream jar, what'll I do? . . .

Fly's in the sugar bowl, shoo fly shoo . . .

Cow's in the cornfield, moo moo moo . . .

Little red wagon, paint it blue . . .

Lost my partner, what'll I do? . . .

I'll get another one prettier than you . . .

Off to Texas, two-by-two . . .

MOVE TO IT!

This song comes in handy at parties. Everybody but one person chooses partners and holds hands. The couples then stand around forming a big circle. The extra person stands in the middle and sings the verse, *Lost my partner, what'll I do?* The extra person then chooses a partner for themselves, singing the verse, *I'll get another one prettier than you.* Now the new person left without a partner has a turn to be in the middle.

There's a Hole in the Bucket

Traditional

There's a hole in the buck - et, Dear

Li - za, Dear Li - za, There's a hole in the buck - et, Dear

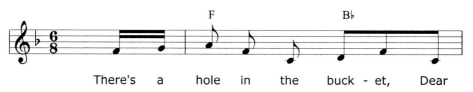

Li - za, a hole. Well, fix it, Dear Hen - ry, Dear

Hen - ry, Dear Hen - ry, Well, fix it, Dear Hen - ry, Dear

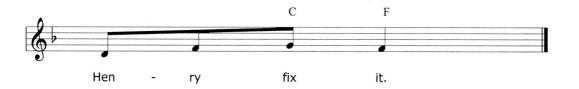

Hen - ry fix it.

88

Learn More About It!

You might wonder why Liza would suggest a stone, of all things, to sharpen the knife. A whetstone (pronounced "wet-stone") is a stone commonly used for sharpening metal-edged tools like axes, knives, and saws.

Sing More About It!

The verses to this traditional German song are like a circle. You end up right where you started!

So fix it, Dear Henry . . .

With what shall I fix it? Dear Liza . . .   *With a stick, Dear Henry . . .*

The stick is too big, Dear Liza . . .   *Then cut it, Dear Henry . . .*

With what shall I cut it? Dear Liza . . .   *With a knife, Dear Henry . . .*

The knife is too dull, Dear Liza . . .   *Then sharpen it, Dear Henry . . .*

With what shall I sharpen it? Dear Liza . . .   *With a stone, Dear Henry . . .*

The stone is too dry, Dear Liza . . .   *Then wet it, Dear Henry . . .*

With what shall I wet it? Dear Liza . . .   *With water, Dear Henry . . .*

With what shall I carry the water? Dear Liza . . .   *With the bucket, Dear Henry . . .*

There's a hole in the bucket!

This Land is Your Land

Woody Guthrie

This land is your land, ____ This land is

my land, ____ From Cal - i - for - nia ____ to the New York

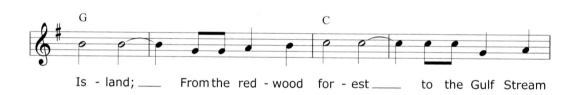

Is - land; ____ From the red - wood for - est ____ to the Gulf Stream

wa - ters ____ This land was made for you and me. ____

Words and Music by Woody Guthrie
TRO - © Copyright 1956 (Renewed) 1958 (Renewed) 1970
(Renewed) 1972 (Renewed) Ludlow Music, Inc., New York, NY
Used by Permission

LEARN MORE ABOUT IT!

Woody Guthrie first wrote this song in 1940, but over the next decade he made changes. The original refrain was *God blessed America for me.* He later changed it to *This land was made for you and me.*

SING MORE ABOUT IT!

As I was walking that ribbon of highway,
I saw above me that endless skyway:
I saw below me that golden valley:
This land was made for you and me.

I've roamed and rambled and I followed my
   footsteps
To the sparkling sands of her diamond deserts;
And all around me a voice was sounding:
This land was made for you and me.

When the sun came shining, and I was
   strolling,
And the wheat fields waving and the dust
   clouds rolling,
As the fog was lifting, a voice was chanting:
This land was made for you and me.

As I went walking, I saw a sign there,
And on the sign it said "No Trespassing."
But on the other side it didn't say nothing,
That side was made for you and me.

In the shadow of the steeple, I saw my people,
By the relief office I seen my people;
As they stood there hungry, I stood there asking,
Is this land made for you and me?

Nobody living can ever stop me,
As I go walking that freedom highway;
Nobody living can ever make me turn back,
This land was made for you and me.

READ MORE ABOUT IT!

This Land Is Your Land by Woody Guthrie, illustrated by Kathy Jakobsen

This Little Light of Mine

Traditional

This lit-tle light of mine, I'm gon-na let it

shine. This lit-tle light of mine, I'm gon-na let it

shine. This lit-tle light of mine, I'm gon-na let it

shine. Let it shine! Let it shine! Let it shine!

Learn More About It!

In the 1950s and 1960s, when African Americans were struggling for their civil rights, this *gospel,* or religious song, could be heard at marches, rallies, and vigils. One of the great things about this song is that it can be sung for a few minutes or stretched out to last much longer.

Sing More About It!

One singer begins and others join in, adding harmony, energy, and new verses.

Hide it under a bushel, No!
I'm gonna let it shine.

Everywhere I go,
I'm gonna let it shine.

Shine all over [add the name of your hometown, school, etc.]
I'm gonna let it shine.

This Old Man

Traditional

This old man, he played one,

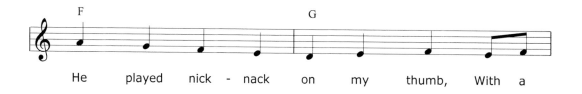

He played nick - nack on my thumb, With a

nick - nack pad - dy whack, give the dog a bone,

This old man came roll - ing home.

Learn More About It!

One of the fun things about this song is that it sings just as well, if not better, without instruments. Try keeping the beat by clapping your hands or tapping your feet. And if anyone knows what a nick-nack or a paddy whack is, please let us know!

Sing More About It!

Here are the verses up to ten. Use these or try making up your own.

He played two, he played nick-nack on my shoe.

He played three, he played nick-nack on my knee.

He played four, he played nick-nack on the door.

He played five, he played nick-nack on a hive.

He played six, he played nick-nack on some sticks.

He played seven, he played nick-nack up to heaven.

He played eight, he played nick-nack on my gate.

He played nine, he played nick-nack on a dime.

He played ten, he played nick-nack once again.

Three Blind Mice

Traditional

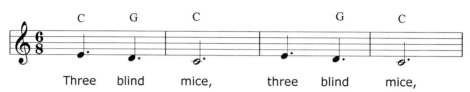

Three   blind   mice,   three   blind   mice,

See   how   they   run!   See   how   they   run!   They

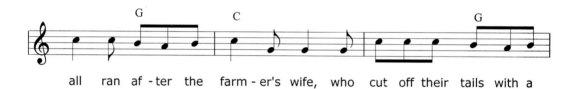

all   ran   af - ter   the   farm - er's   wife,   who   cut   off   their   tails   with   a

carv - ing   knife.   Did   you   ev - er   see   such   a

sight   in   your   life   as   three   blind   mice.

Learn More about it!

It's said this song was first sung in England, and that the "farmer's wife" is actually Queen Mary I (famously known as Bloody Mary).

Did you know?

Mice are quite popular in England. In fact, there's even a National Mouse Club that dates back more than a hundred years. The club promotes the exhibition of "fancy" mice. Imagine winning a blue ribbon at the mouse show!

Sing More about it!

This song is often sung as a *round*. You can try singing the round in two groups, or have individual singers join in, one after the other.

Group One
Three blind mice, three blind mice,
See how they run, See how they run,
They all ran after the farmer's wife
Who cut off their tails with a carving knife,
Did you ever see such a sight in your life
As three blind mice.

Group Two
(wait out this first line)
Three blind mice, three blind mice,
See how they run, See how they run,
They all ran after the farmer's wife
Who cut off their tails with a carving knife,
Did you ever see such a sight in your life
As three blind mice.

TRAIN IS A COMIN'

Traditional

Train is a com - in', oh yes.

Train is a com - in', oh yes.

Train is a com - in', train is a com - in', ____

train is a com - in', oh yes.

Learn More about it!

Some say the train in this old spiritual refers to a train on the Underground Railroad. The Underground Railroad wasn't really underground nor was it a railroad. It was a series of "safe" houses before the Civil War set up by people called Abolitionists, who wanted to free the slaves. The houses stretched from the South all the way to the North. Tens of thousands of slaves gained their freedom using this secret network, including Harriet Tubman, who later guided hundreds of slaves to freedom.

Sing More about it!

There are endless possibilities for this song. Think about all the things you might do getting ready for the train. Then make up your own verses!

Better get your ticket, oh yes.

Room for many more, oh yes.

Here comes the conductor, oh yes.

Better pack your bags, oh yes.

You can even change the mode of transportation!

School bus is a comin', oh yes.

Carpool is a comin', oh yes.

TWINKLE, TWINKLE LiTTLE STaR

Traditional

Twin - kle, twin - kle lit - tle star, How I won - der

what you are. Up a - bove the world so high,

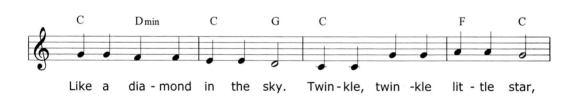

Like a dia - mond in the sky. Twin - kle, twin -kle lit - tle star,

How I won - der what you are.

Learn More About It!

Have you ever wondered what a star is? Stars are balls of very hot gas, usually made up of hydrogen and helium, the two lightest gases. These gases are constantly exploding and burning. That's what makes a star "shine." The hottest stars are white. Medium stars (like our sun) are yellow. The coolest stars are red. It can take billions of years for a star to burn up all of its fuel.

Two for One!

While many people believe "Twinkle, Twinkle Little Star" was written by a very young Wolfgang Amadeus Mozart, Mozart actually composed Twelve Variations on the traditional melody. The tune is based on an eighteenth-century French folk song called "Ah! Vous dirais-je, Maman." The original words were not about stars at all, but about a child wanting candy! Try humming the tune. Do any other popular songs come to mind? What if you use the words below?

Baa, baa, black sheep, have you any wool?	*A-B-C-D-E-F-G,*
Yes, sir, yes, sir,	*H-I-J-K,*
Three bags full.	*L-M-N-O-P,*
One for my master,	*Q-R-S,*
One for my dame,	*T-U-V,*
One for the little boy who lives down the lane.	*W-X-Y and Z.*
	Now I know my ABCs,
Baa, baa, black sheep, have you any wool?	*Next time won't you sing with me!*
Yes, sir, yes, sir, three bags full.	

We Wish You a Merry Christmas

Traditional

We wish you a mer-ry Christ-mas, We

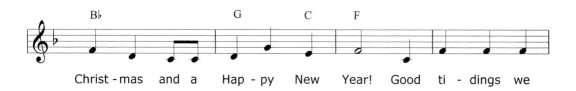

wish you a mer-ry Christ-mas, We wish you a mer-ry

Christ-mas and a Hap-py New Year! Good ti-dings we

bring to you and your kin, Good ti-dings for

Christ-mas and a Hap-py New Year!

Learn More about it!

This Christmas carol was sung in England as early as the sixteenth century. Back then, carolers sang for sweets and a few spare coins. Figgy pudding was a favorite Christmas dessert.

Sing More about it!

Now bring us some figgy pudding,
Now bring us some figgy pudding,
Now bring us some figgy pudding,
And bring it right here.

We won't go until we get some,
We won't go until we get some,
We won't go until we get some,
So bring it right here!

Cook it!

If you're interested in trying this Christmas treat, have an adult help you with this recipe.

FIGGY PUDDING

1 cup bread crumbs
½ cup flour
1 cup chopped figs
¼ cup light brown sugar
½ teaspoon salt
1 teaspoon baking powder
½ teaspoon cinnamon
½ teaspoon nutmeg
1 teaspoon lemon rind
1 beaten egg
milk

Mix together all of the dry ingredients. Add the egg. Add enough milk so that the mixture is moist, but not runny. Now you have pudding. Pour into a greased mold and steam over boiling water for 2 hours.

What Shall We Do?

Traditional

What shall we do when we all go out,

all go out, all go out? What shall we do when we

all go out, When we all go out to play?

Learn More About It!

What do you like to do when you go outside? The answer might be different whether you live in a big city, a smaller neighborhood, or in the country. In the city you might like to go to the park. In the country you might like to go fishing. Wherever you live, you might like to play catch, ride bikes, or walk your dog.

Sing More About It!

Here are a few possibilities, but you can always make up your own.

I'll ride a bike when we all go out,
All go out, all go out,
I'll ride a bike when we all go out,
When we all go out to play.

I'll play a game when we all go out . . .

I'll catch a ball when we all go out . . .

I'll jump a rope when we all go out . . .

The Wheels on the Bus

Traditional

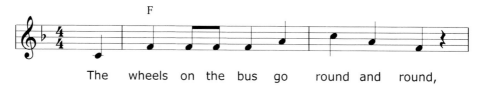

The   wheels   on   the   bus   go   round   and   round,

round and round,   round and round. The   wheels on   the   bus   go

round   and   round,   all   through   the   town.

LEARN MORE ABOUT IT!

There are many kinds of buses—school buses, tour buses, and city buses, but only school buses are allowed to be painted yellow. Yellow is an easy color to see, even in bad weather like rain, snow, and fog. The particular shade of yellow on school buses has a special name: National School Bus Chrome Yellow. In most states, it is illegal to use a vehicle painted school-bus yellow for anything other than a school bus. That means, if you buy a secondhand school bus, you better repaint it a different color!

SING MORE ABOUT IT!

This song has a lot of verses. If you get through these, try making up your own!

The wipers on the bus go swish, swish, swish . . .

The doors on the bus go open and shut . . .

The driver on the bus says, "Move on back!" . . .

The people on the bus go up and down . . .

The babies on the bus go "Waa! Waa! Waa!" . . .

The mamas on the bus go "Shh! Shh! Shh!" . . .

MOVE TO IT!

Each of the verses in this song has a movement. For instance, for the wheels going round and round, move your hands in circles, one around the other. For the verse with the babies, wipe your eyes like you're crying. You get the idea.

READ MORE ABOUT IT!

The Wheels on the Bus (a pop-up book) by Paul O. Zelinsky
The Seals on the Bus by Lenny Hort

When The Saints Go Marching In

Traditional

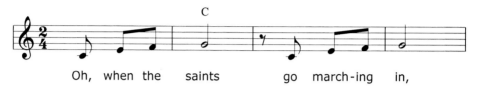

Oh, when the saints go march-ing in,

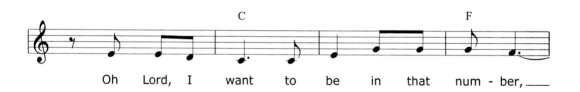

Oh, when the saints go march - ing in,

Oh Lord, I want to be in that num - ber, ____

____ When the saints go march - ing in.

Learn More about it!

This song is a *spiritual*. A spiritual is a religious song that is more energetic than a hymn. Spirituals were first sung by African Americans in the southern United States. Just as in this song, many spirituals talk of a time in the future when people will be free of their everyday troubles.

Sing More about it!

Oh, when the sun begins to shine,
Oh, when the sun begins to shine,
Oh Lord, I want to be in that number,
When the sun begins to shine.

Oh, when the trumpet sounds its call,
Oh, when the trumpet sounds its call,
Oh Lord, I want to be in that number,
When the trumpet sounds its call.

YANKEE DOODLE

Traditional

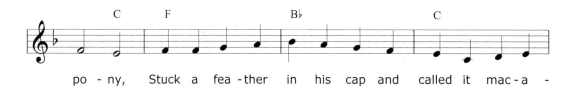

Yan - kee Doo - dle went to town a - rid - ing on a

po - ny, Stuck a fea -ther in his cap and called it mac - a -

ro - ni. Yan - kee Doo - dle keep it up, Yan - kee Doo - dle Dan - dy.

Mind the mu - sic and the step and with the girls be han - dy.

Learn More about it!

This patriotic song has been popular for generations. Today, it even serves as the state song for Connecticut. The words we know today are said to be written by a British doctor named Richard Schuckburg. When he wrote them he was making fun of the ragtag uniforms of the American colonists during the French and Indian War.

When the song talks about Yankee Doodle sticking a feather in his cap and calling it "macaroni," it refers not to a noodle, but to a fancy Italian style of dress popular at the time. "Doodle" meant a kind of fool, while "Dandy" meant a kind of fancy-pants personality. Strangely enough, the song later became a favorite rallying cry for the colonists during the American Revolutionary War.

Sing More about it!

This song has many verses. Some people say close to two hundred! Here are a couple to get you started on making up your own.

Father and I went down to camp along with Captain Gooding
And there we saw the men and boys as thick as hasty pudding.

There was Colonel Washington upon a strapping stallion,
Giving orders to his men, I guess there was a million.

ABOUT THE AUTHORS

Paul DuBois Jacobs and Jennifer Swender are a husband-and-wife writing team who live in Brooklyn, New York. Paul has coauthored four books with musician Pete Seeger: *Pete Seeger's Storytelling Book, Abiyoyo Returns, Some Friends to Feed: The Story of Stone Soup,* and *Deaf Musicians.* Jennifer is an elementary school teacher and curriculum developer. They are also the authors of *My Subway Ride.*